Why Then The Law?

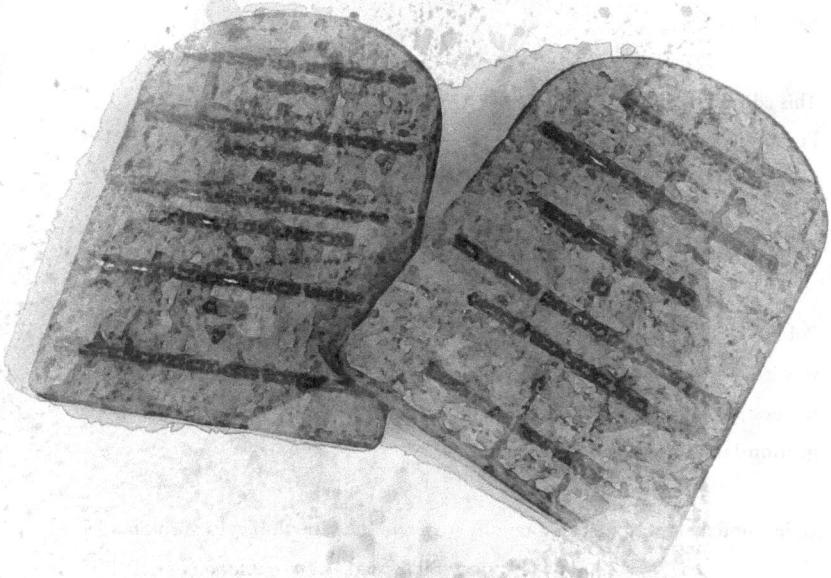

R.L. Watson

Why Then the law?

This edition published 2023 by
Pronomian Publishing LLC
Chatsworth, GA 30705

ISBN: 979-8-9851529-7-5

Cover Design: Jeromy Kusch (Lanternministry.org)

Why Then The Law?

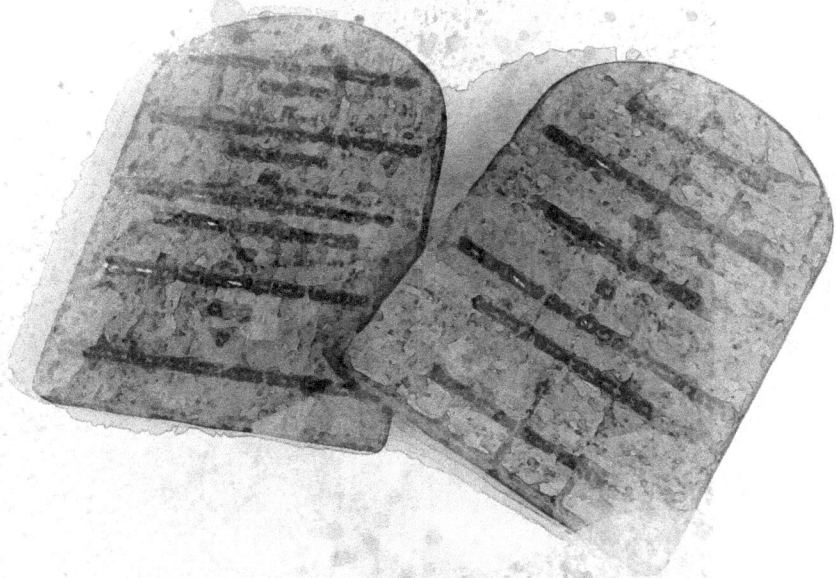

R.L. Watson

To Dad.

Thanks for teaching me that life is more complex than one-dimensional answers.

CONTENTS

INTRODUCTION

THE LAW AND THE SCARECROW

Accuracy of observation is the equivalent of accuracy of thinking.[1]

Any investigation into any topic requires an accurate perspective of what is being studied. If one wants to correctly understand how something works, or even evaluate if something is a good option, they need all the facts. Now, of course, no one can have perfect knowledge, but enough information beyond a one-dimensional evaluation is attainable. This is true of a new car, a global issue, health insurance, mortgage contact, or even a diet. Informed opinions are important.

Any parent will tell you that children are the worst at this. They will look at a piece of food and decide that they hate it simply because of its colour. Typically, the conversations go like this:

"It's disgusting…"

"You haven't even tried it. You'll like it."

"No. It's yucky…"

Luckily, most of my children are either in or approaching their teenage years and eat pretty much anything and everything, but it is a

---

1   Wallace Stevens, *Opus Posthumous* (New York: Vintage Books, 1989), 185.

frustration many parents go through. As people grow up, some move on from this kind of reasoning, while others persist with negativity biases; they just apply them to bigger issues such as politics, economics, and religion. Rather than wanting to understand all the elements of any given issue, they hold onto one narrow aspect of it, form a conclusion, and fight for it. This approach is problematic because such limited understandings result in hasty reactions and narrow assumptions. It also has a detrimental effect on resolving related issues. Using global warming as an example, if someone says that X is the cause and ignores other influences, then their solution to climate change isn't going to be as effective. If we want to understand an issue or topic correctly, we need to investigate and evaluate it accurately, lest we end up setting fire to a straw man.

As followers of Christ, it is important that our theology and our understanding of the character and nature of God is developed and built upon accurate engagement with His Word. Different people may come to different conclusions on different topics, and that is okay. What counts is that we put in the time and effort to consider the totality of God's revealed Word in order to build a more accurate theology, rather than mere proof texts. Proof-texting, when taken to the extreme, can result in the creation of cults and dangerous theologies. However, generally, it's applied to secondary or adiaphorous matters that aren't overly significant and shouldn't cause any disunity. The topic of this book falls into this category. While I know of many people who disagree with me on the role of the Law in Christianity, I happily call them brothers and sisters in Christ because we are still united in our agreement with the Gospel. Their disagreement is not the issue I am addressing here. The issue of concern is the nature of the discussions about the topic, and how they arrived at that conclusion.

In my experience, the problem I have observed with most critiques of the Law is that they are usually straw man arguments that attack caricatures of the Law and ignore what much of scripture has to say about it, with appeals to what Luther or the Protestant tradition would think (at least their understanding of those things).

The anti-Semitic polemic of some of the early Church Fathers, who called the Law a punishment and curse on "those evil Jews," have passed down many of these caricatures to us. There are also those in church history who said that the Law is so antithetical to the Gospel that it should have no relevance whatsoever to the believer. Although this is beginning to shift, this latter thought is more common today and arises when one considers the individual commandments in isolation from their context in Scripture. Rather than seeing our obedience to the commandments as demonstrations of love and gratitude for redemption in a covenantal, relational setting, many have described the commandments as legalistic burdens. Consequently, there is a belief that the "Old Covenant" is based on performance and entirely void of grace.

However, even a cursory glance at the Old Testament will reveal many instances of grace and forgiveness independent of obedience, performance, and conformity. Although the Mosaic Covenant does say there are consequences for disobedience, this is a principle shared by the New Testament as well. Consider Ananias and Sapphira (Acts 5:5, 10), the greedy believers in Corinth (1 Cor. 11:30), and the recipients of the letter to the Hebrews (Heb. 12:7), to name a few. Consider too how the descriptions in Psalms 19 and 119, for example, betray the cold misrepresentations of the Law by portraying it as desirable and precious—an idea echoed by Paul in Romans. Also, in Psalm 31 and 51, we find David experiencing forgiveness from the Lord independent of sacrifice. Some may try to claim that before Jesus forgiveness and righteousness were based on obedience and ritual, but that is clearly not the case. Unfortunately, we have inherited a poor hermeneutic and opinion of what is inaccurately called "the Old Testament"[2] from those who were genuinely trying to preserve the Gospel. But in their zeal, they erred, and as a result, many discussions on the nature and purpose of the Law seem to be overly simplistic, missing its more complicated role and function.

In this book, I want to explore the Law's origin and nature to help us better understand its purpose, thereby enabling us to have greater clarity regarding how it functions as a covenant obligation. A Christian's theology matters because truth matters. God is a God of truth, and love rejoices in the truth (1 Cor. 13:6). Therefore, we should pursue the truth. We should seek to see the Law, not according to caricatures painted by our spiritual forefathers, but according to what God says about it. But more importantly, although still related to the pursuit of truth, the glory and honour of God needs to be upheld. Because the Law is a revelation of who God is, to deride the Law is a slight on His character. This is why 1 John says that obeying the Law is how we show our love for our creator, the Law-giver (1 John 5:2-3).

It is my hope that by the end of this book, you would have thought biblically, meaningfully, and deeply about the Law of God. I also hope that you will come away with a fresh appreciation of the goodness of the Law, and an understanding of why David and Paul could speak so highly of it.

---

2   See R.L. Watson, *Forgotten Covenant* (Port Orchard, WA: Ark House Press, 2021), 11-13.

CHAPTER 1
ORIGINS OF THE LAW

This is what I mean: the law, which came 430 years afterward,
does not annul a covenant previously ratified by God, so as to
make the promise void.
—Galatians 3:17

In my view, rightly understanding the nature and role of the Torah requires acknowledging that the Law expressed in the Mosaic covenant was not a brand-new revelation at Mt Sinai. Granted, some aspects of the Law were contextualised for the nation of Abraham's descendants, such as the judicial and sacrificial regulations, but the core elements and key features were there from the beginning.

Charles Ryrie, however, would disagree. In his book *Dispensationalism*, he explains that within each chapter of history, "God introduces new things for which man becomes responsible."[1] Thus, according to this view, the Law revealed at Sinai was a 'new thing,' and it was only *after* this point in history that humanity was expected to adhere to that code. Thus, "...prior to the giving of the law, people were obviously not held responsible for something that did not exist."[2] While this proposition makes sense according to the framework of Dispensationalism, how does it measure up to the teaching of Scripture?

---

1   Charles C. Ryrie, *Dispensationalism* (Chicago : Moody Press, 1995), 33.
2   Ibid., 34.

Ancient Origins

A key passage that speaks quite strongly against this dispensationalist idea is found in Paul's letter to the Romans:

> ...just as sin came into the world through one man, and death through sin, and so death spread to all men because all sinned - for sin indeed was in the world before the law was given, but sin is not counted where there is no law. Yet death reigned from Adam to Moses.
> —Romans 5:12-14

Although this passage says nothing explicit about the Law's existence prior to Moses, it can be logically and exegetically inferred from the text. This passage says that "sin is not counted where there is no law," which means that sin's existence requires the Law's existence. As Paul wrote earlier in Romans, "For the law brings wrath, but where there is no law there is no transgression" (Rom. 4:15). We see this elsewhere in the New Testament when John in his first letter wrote, "sin is lawlessness" (1 John 3:4), or as the King James renders it: "sin is the transgression of the law." Therefore, if the Law did not exist before Moses, then no one before Moses sinned. But we know that is not true.

If the Law was non-existent, then God's wrath could not have existed either. Yet events like the flood show that this is not the case. To demonstrate that the Law's origins pre-date Moses, Paul explains that death, which is the penalty and consequence of sin (Rom. 6:23)—defined by the Law and necessitating the Law's existence—"reigned from Adam to Moses." One only needs to read the oft-repeated phrase in the genealogical passages of early Genesis, "and he died" to see this. Therefore, as Phillip Griffiths explains, this portion in Romans 5 teaches us that,

> In pre-Mosaic times, although the law of God was not explicitly revealed, it was nevertheless a reality, people know the difference between right and wrong, demonstrating that 'the work of the law is written on their hearts' (Rom 2:15).[3]

The only consistent conclusion one can draw from this passage in Romans 5 is that the presence of sin and death means that God's Law was a real and active standard prior to Moses.

The nature of the revelation of the Law is kind of like experience of the Pevensie children in *The Lion, The Witch and the Wardrobe* (and consequently the reader). They don't learn about The Deep Magic, which declares that a traitor is to be put to death, until a later point of the narrative when the Witch reminds Aslan of it. Although Chapter Thirteen is its first mention, it is obviously a concept that existed prior to that point in that world. The narrative merely brings it up because the context calls for a "reminder."

This principle can also be illustrated in the film *The Wizard of Oz.* This movie is historically significant because it was one of the first to be filmed in colour, and its success ensured the future of Technicolour. Moreover, many who saw the film after its release at the theatre had possibly not seen a live-action movie filmed in colour before. I remember when my boys were watching it for the first time. I paused it just before Dorothy leaves the house and enters into the World of Oz. I got them to imagine that they had only ever seen black and

---

3   Phillip D. R. Griffiths, *Covenant Theology: A Reformed Baptist Perspective* (Eugene, OR: Resource Publications, 2022), 39.

white movies before that moment so that when they saw the bright and colourful Munchkin City, they could understand its significance. Was the world black and white before colour film and photography? I'm sure many young children have wondered if "the olden days" were only black and white because that is all that is recorded in film and photographs. However, we know that the world was not in black and white; it is just that technology was unable to capture colour back then. In a similar sense, the fact that we do not find any explicit mention of a list of laws until Exodus does not mean that God's Law did not exist prior to Exodus. As the passage in Romans 5 demonstrates, as do many other places we will consider below, the Law was indeed a real standard to which humanity was held accountable prior to Moses.

Historic Accountability

One only needs to read the prehistoric and patriarchal narratives in Genesis to see the Lord holding people accountable for sins that were not defined textually until the giving of the Law through Moses. If there was no Law, how could God be just by counting people as guilty for disobeying a non-existent Law? Consider the following examples:

There is Cain's murder of Abel specifically, as well as humanity's violence against one another in general, which led to the flood.

God rebuked Abimelech for adultery (Gen. 20:3-9), and Joseph called adultery a sin (Gen. 39:7-9).

We read in Genesis 15 that Abram's descendants would be the instrument by which God would remove the inhabitants of Canaan for their *abominations*. It is not until Leviticus 18:21-17 that these abominations are formally defined as sexual immorality. No doubt this condemnation also included idolatry and human sacrifice, which are likewise prohibited by the Law.

Also consider the sexual immorality and oppression of the poor (actions condemned by the Law) committed by the inhabitants of Sodom and Gomorrah prior to their annihilation in Genesis 19. What is fascinating about this is that here we find nations outside of God's line of promise being held accountable to His holy standard.

There is also the matter of how Cain's offering was rejected while Abel's was accepted. The interesting thing is not only that there existed a standard of sacrifice that they were to adhere to, but also the fact that they were sacrificing at all. The Bible says nothing regarding where the idea of sacrifice came from, how they knew about it, or how to do it (a detail that would not come until Moses). Its practice is just assumed.

Then there is Noah, who is told to take two of each type of animal and seven pairs of every kind of clean animal (Gen. 7:2). There is nothing in the Noahic narrative that explicitly speaks to whether unclean animals were prohibited for eating. In fact, the command to eat meat in Genesis 9:3 is quite general in its scope, and any evaluation about whether Leviticus 11 could be implied back into Genesis 9 is outside the scope of this book. But the point is those categories of clean and unclean existed prior to Moses, and at the very least provided the conceptual seed and foundation for the food restrictions of Leviticus 11. Moreover, the reader finds that, following the flood, Noah specifically sacrificed only clean animals on an altar. Just like the sacrifices of Cain and Able, what makes an animal clean or unclean is not explained, nor is it a concept explicitly explained to Noah or the reader until Sinai. And even then, all that is explained in Leviticus is how to identify it, not why. Nonetheless, categories of clean and unclean are just assumed.

On the other side of these condemnations, we see God's approval of Abraham, saying to Jacob that he "obeyed My voice and kept My charge (*mismarti*), My commandments (*miswotay*), My statutes (*huqqotay*), and My laws (*terotay*)" (Gen. 26:5). In Deuteronomy 11:1, with one variant, these same words are used to describe the obligations of the Mosaic Covenant to which the people were to be faithful: "You shall therefore love the Lord your God and keep his charge (*mismarti*), his statutes (*huqqotay*), his rules (*mispataw*), and his commandments (*miswotay*)." Although terotay is not repeated in Deuteronomy 11:1, its root is the word Torah ("Law"), which appears in the singular form in passages such as Jeremiah 31:33 as a reference to the Law of God in the context of Israel's breaking of the Covenant. Given its pre-existence, this passage in Genesis 26 shows that the Law of God is the standard of blamelessness that Abraham was charged to keep in Genesis 17.

Therefore, since we find that the Law of God is an eternal, albeit somewhat abstract, standard that is intertwined with the character of the Lord, the Law is clearly external to the Mosaic Covenant. And what we find in Exodus 19:5, with the imperative to obey God, and the outlining of commandments from Exodus 20 onward, is the official and formal incorporation and contextualisation of the pre-existing Law into the pre-existing covenant with Abraham that Israel participated in. Consequently, although the two are related, the Law is not synonymous with the Mosaic Covenant. And to talk about them as being the same is to ignore what scripture says about the Law's true nature and origin.

This does raise a significant question: if the Law existed prior to Sinai and it was on the consciences of people, why wait until Moses for its formal revelation? Or as Paul asks in Galatians, "why then the law?" (Gal. 3:19). In our next chapter, we will look at this question and the complexity of its answer.

CHAPTER 2
PURPOSES OF THE LAW

Things danced on the screen do not look the way they do on the stage. On the stage, dancing is three-dimensional, but a motion-picture is two-dimensional.[1]

Like a diamond, life is complex and multifaceted. Sure, we can simplify our lives, and summarise them into simple ideas and descriptions, but it is more than just one thing. There is pain, celebration, loss, and joy. There is peace and there is conflict. Sometimes there is joy in suffering and regret in gain. Consider too our purposes. In my life, I am a husband, a father, a brother, a teacher, a writer, a friend, and a servant of Christ. While all that I do can be summarised as worshipping Him (Col. 3:17), what I do and how I relate to others are shaped and defined by each purpose and context. Although Gene Kelly in the quote above was lamenting about the lack of depth in cinematic representations of dancing, the same can be said about two-dimensional representations of life whereby concepts and issues are oversimplified. When directors ignore the complexity of people and issues, the audience is presented with stereotypes and predictable archetypes that seem to offer solutions to problems that would never work in reality. It is almost a cinematic straw man on life. We cannot take a topic and flatten it with a steamroller to create a simplistic, two-dimensional image.

This is especially true when it comes to our theology and interpretation of Scripture. When we oversimplify things in God's word,

---

1   Gene Kelly. Quoted in New York Times, Feb 03,1996.

we do not just create a straw man theology and misrepresent ideas but we also rob God's word of its beauty and complexity. Unfortunately, when it comes to discussions and descriptions of God's Law, many describe it as a curse from which we have to be set free. However, when we actually look at the breadth of what Scripture says about the Torah, we get a much different picture of its complexity and beauty.

When most people explain what the Law's purpose is, they say it is to reveal sin and demonstrate one's need for salvation. And indeed, it does have this purpose, but to say this is its only purpose is overly simplistic and ignores the broader nature and overall intent of the Law. There is, rather, a variety of purposes and functions of the Law that can help make sense of why God waited until Moses to manifest His Law in the way that He did.

To Deal with Sin

In Galatians, Paul writes that the Law "was added because of transgressions" (Gal 3:19). But what exactly does this mean? As seen in the previous chapter, due to the Law's ancient origins and the nature of sin, this cannot mean that the Law was brought into existence and delivered to His people because they were being bad and needed some rules to make them better. Without the Law and commandments, by what standard does one define "bad" anyway? Rather, the Law was *formally* added to the Covenants of promise (Gal. 3:17-18) because of sin. Due to the corruption of the human condition that came as a result of the fall, the Law needed to be made explicit for His covenant people as an act of grace. As to what this means and how this works, there are two prominent interpretations to consider. First, R.C Sproul in a sermon on Galatians 3:15-20 explains that the Law was not formally given and revealed until Sinai because people's consciences had not been sufficiently weakened and seared through sin until that point. As he elaborates on this condition:

> In pre-Mosaic times, although the law of God was not
> explicitly revealed, it was nevertheless a reality, people know
> the difference between right and wrong, demonstrating that
> 'the work of the law is written on their hearts' (Rom 2:15).[2]

This, according to Sproul, is the meaning of Galatians 3:19: "the law… was added because the accumulation of transgressions and their effects, required its explicit communication."[3]

Another interpretation of this verse says that the Law was added to the Abrahamic and Mosaic Covenant as a revelation of Christ and His ministry. According to Tim Hegg in his commentary on Galatians, the Greek word for "because of, *charin*, "indicates 'the goal' to which something points or proceeds."[4] For example, in Jude 1:16 we read: "These are grumblers, malcontents, following their own sinful desires; they are loud-mouthed boasters, showing favoritism to gain (*charin*) advantage." And in Titus 1:5, Paul wrote: "This is why I left you in Crete, so that (*charin*) you might put what remained into order." Thus, the Law explains and reveals in typological form how God was going to deal with sin. More specifically, it reveals the way the sacrifices and priesthood pointed to Christ and His ministry. This would have certainly been a part of Jesus' discussion with the two men on the way to Emmaus (Luke 24:17).

---

2   R.C. Sproul, "The Covenant," *Ligonier Ministries*, Feb, 2017, www.ligonier.org/learn/
     sermons/covenant. C.f. Js 1:23-25.

3   Ibid.

4   Tim Hegg, *Paul's Epistle to the Galatians* (Tacoma, WA: TorahResource, 2010), 148.

I do not think one needs to decide between which interpretation of Galatians 3:19 is correct, as both reflect valid functions of the Law. However, is this *all* that the Law was about? Was this the Law's chief purpose? According to Martin Luther, the Law was given:

> to reveal to a person his sin, blindness, misery, his ignorance, hatred, and contempt of God, his death, hell, and condemnation. This is the principal purpose of the Law and its most valuable contribution. As long as a person is not a murderer, adulterer, thief, he would swear that he is righteous. How is God going to humble such a person except by the Law? The Law is the hammer of death, the thunder of hell, and the lightning of God's wrath to bring down the proud and shameless hypocrites.[5]

This function/purpose is valid, but again, is it the *principal* purpose? Likewise, I have often heard it claimed that in giving the Law, God gave Israel an unassailable goal and standard that they could never meet or measure up to just to show them that they are sinners. But is this the case? I struggle to accept that the chief purpose of God's Law is accusatory and condemning.

Positive Obedience

As a teacher, I establish behaviour expectations in the classroom such as, "students will actively listen and not speak while the teacher is giving information or instructions," and "if it doesn't belong to you, don't touch it without permission." I don't do this just so that I can show students that they are naughty, although the expectations will

---

5   Martin Luther, *Commentary on the Epistle to the Galatians*, 91, Kindle.

highlight that they are, but to allow the smooth running of the class-room and maximise learning. The primary purpose of these expectations, therefore, is positive, not negative. I am sure we could say something similar about the purposes of expectations we as parents would have for our children at home. In the same way, the wider testimony of Scripture describes the Law as being much more than negative. We only need to turn to the book of Deuteronomy after the covenant renewal with the second generation to see this:

> For this commandment that I command you today is not too hard for you, neither is it far off. It is not in heaven, that you should say, 'Who will ascend to heaven for us and bring it to us, that we may hear it and do it?' Neither is it beyond the sea, that you should say, 'Who will go over the sea for us and bring it to us, that we may hear it and do it?' But the word is very near you. It is in your mouth and in your heart, so that you can do it.
> —Deuteronomy 30:11-14

Here, the people are told that the instruction to fulfil the covenant obligations as spelled out in the Law is not impossible to do. Peter Craigie in his commentary on Deuteronomy explains that the Law "not being in the heavens or across the sea" means that it is not so complicated that they cannot understand it. It is not a secret that they cannot know, and that it is not so removed from everyday life that they cannot do it. Compared to the Mesopotamian hero Gilgamesh who crossed the sea in a quest for life, "life was to be found by the Hebrews in the law of the covenant which Moses set before them: *it is in your mouth and in your mind* (lit. 'heart'), *so that you may do it.*[6] Note the given purpose of the Law. It does not say, "so that I can show you your sin or inability." It says, "so that you can *do it*," revealing that God's purpose is tied to His expectation: He expected them to do it and explains that they should be able to do it.

This is also reflected in the way that the Psalmist wrote, "You have commanded your precepts to be kept diligently... Give me understanding that I may keep your law and observe it with my whole heart" (Psalm 119:4, 34). So much of Psalm 119's focus is on the desire to keep the Law, and encouraging its reader to do the same, and not once did they feel burdened by its demands.

Isaiah later demonstrates this attitude towards the Law when reflecting on the people's disobedience. He laments, "Was it not the Lord, against whom we have sinned, in whose ways they would not walk, and whose law they would not obey?" (Isaiah 42:24). Note that Isaiah does not say "could not,"[7] but instead says "would not." The Hebrew, *abah*, means to be willing or to consent to something. For example, in Judges, Jephthah recounts to the King of the Ammonites that the King of Edom "would not listen" nor consent (*abah*) to Israel's request to pass through his land. The issue here with Israel's disobedience was not so much about ability; it was more about willingness. Isaiah's emphasis on the will reflects how humanity's fallen nature has corrupted their will and desire to be obedient (Rom. 8:7).

Nonetheless, some people in the Bible are described as blameless. These are the ones who, despite falling short, respond as the Law prescribes: with confession and demonstration of contrition. In this

---

6   Peter Craigie, *The Book of Deuteronomy*, NICOT (Grand Rapids: Eerdmans, 1976), 365.

7   Heb. *yakol*. Be able, have power. E.g. "Then Joseph could not [*yakol*] control himself before all those who stood by him" (Gen 45:1).

way, despite violating the Law, they have in a sense still kept it. This was the standard that was achievable in those verses from Deuteronomy, and the expectation here in Isaiah. Not flawless observance, but a willingness to obey. That is where the Gospel comes in. All the same, the fact that the fall has hindered one's ability to obey does not change the Law's original purpose. God places the emphasis on the people's willingness, and the fact that the law is made simple so that they can do it reveals that the Law's primary purpose is to give people a standard to be obeyed.

Although the Law does expose sinfulness, this is a secondary intent. If it were its primary purpose, then that would be putting the cart before the horse. Could you imagine if we said that the purpose of human rights laws is to expose human rights violations, not to ensure people's well-being is preserved? That would be nonsensical. The same is true of God's Law. As we saw in our discussion earlier about Romans 5, sin is a failure to meet the standard of God's righteousness, as revealed in the Law, and thus the expectation of obedience must precede the condemnation that follows the failure to uphold it. And so, if the Law came before sin, which logically it must, its original and therefore primary purpose is to be a standard for people to conform to.

Thus, a significant reason the Lord did not reveal the Law explicitly in Scripture until this point was because of the purposes of the Mosaic Covenant. As will be explained in more detail below, the descendants of Abraham were to be a Kingdom of Priests and a light to the nations, which was a part of the restoration of humanity's vocation as defined in God's act of creation, and the Law supported and promoted this goal, for it describes what it looks like to live out this role. And since this is the case, God's purpose is clearly that He wants people to obey it.

The Bringer of Life

As the remainder of the chapter will highlight, the many promises of blessing for obedience further emphasises that God's Law is a standard to be obeyed, not simply something that exists only to reveal sin, nor something to be feared.

Far from being a terrible burden, there are many parts of Scripture that give positive depictions of the Law. This is especially true in passages like Psalm 19:7-8, which declares: "The law of the Lord is perfect, reviving the soul; the testimony of the Lord is sure, making wise the simple; the precepts of the Lord are right, rejoicing the heart..." Many more are found in Psalm 119. For instance:

> In the way of your testimonies I delight, as much as in all riches. I will meditate on your precepts, and fix my eyes on your ways. I will delight in your statutes; I will not forget your word...
> —Psalm 119:14-16

> The insolent smear me with lies, but with my whole heart I keep your precepts; their heart is unfeeling like fat, but I delight in your law. It is good for me that I was afflicted, that I might learn your statutes. The law of your mouth is better to me than thousands of gold and silver pieces.
> —Psalm 119:69-72

And even Moses himself, as he spoke to the congregation before they entered the Promised Land, said:

> I call heaven and earth to witness against you today, that I have set before you life and death, blessing and curse. There-

fore choose life, that you and your offspring may live, loving
the Lord your God, obeying his voice and holding fast to
him, for he is your life and length of days, that you may dwell
in the land that the Lord swore to your fathers, to Abraham,
to Isaac, and to Jacob, to give them.
—Deuteronomy 30:19-20

According to this passage, the "curse" is not the Law, the act of giving the Law, nor the Law's expectations. Rather, the curse lies in the disobedience and rejection of the Law. Obedience and embracing God's Law is equated with life and blessing. This is why Paul was able to say that the Law "is holy, and the commandment is holy and righteous and good" (Rom. 7:12). Together, these verses paint a picture of the Law as a life-giving blessing instead of condemning accusation.

While obedience is the Law's primary purpose, the larger, and what I consider to be the predominant aims of the Law, belong to its revelatory nature. These revelatory functions are the three, main, interrelated, positive purposes that allow the covenant people of God to be a light to the nations.

Theological Revelation

Another significant purpose of the Law is that it serves as a revelation of God's holiness, righteousness, and justice. Murder is wrong because He is the light of life and the God of the living. It is also wrong because humanity belongs to Him and thus murder is theft and vandalism of God's property. Idolatry is wrong because He is the one true God. Adultery is wrong because God is faithful. Justice needs to be fair and right because He is the God of truth and the perfect judge. As Jeffrey, Ovey, and Sachs put it: "God's law... is not external to him, but intrinsic, reflecting his own perfect righteousness and holiness. To obey God's law is to obey God."[8] One only needs to read the often-repeated phrase throughout the Law after the giving of many commandments, "Be holy, *for* I am holy," to see this. The Law, therefore, contains instructions, commandments, and prohibitions that are based on the Lord's own character and nature.

This means that the Law is not the cultural product of some ancient religion or the exclusive property of one people group. It reveals God as the creator, promise keeper, protector, provider and deliverer to name a few. One of the clearest examples of this can be found in the way the autobiographical prologue in Exodus 20 connects the Decalogue to God's self-revelation as a summary of what has gone before and the expression of His will. Consequently, obedience to these laws is not only a demonstration that the individual belongs to the Lord but also is a revelation to the world of what God is like. This by-product is why Moses could tell the people in Deuteronomy:

> I have taught you statutes and rules, as the Lord my God
> commanded me, that you should do them in the land that
> you are entering to take possession of it. Keep them and do
> them, for that will be your wisdom and your understanding
> in the sight of the peoples, who, when they hear all these
> statutes, will say, 'Surely this great nation is a wise and
> understanding people.' For what great nation is there that has
> a god so near to it as the Lord our God is to us, whenever we
> call upon him? And what great nation is there, that has

---

8   Steve Jeffrey, Mike Ovey, & Andrew Sach, *Pierced for our Transgressions* (Nottingham: IVP, 2007), 302.

statutes and rules so righteous as all this law that I set before
you today?
—Deuteronomy 4:5-8

Expressions of Love

God also gave the Law to explain how covenant members are to
respond to and relate to Him. Namely, like a marriage vow, obedience
to the Law's precepts and statutes is a demonstration of one's love and
gratitude to their creator and redeemer. It was never about God saying,
as some try to claim, "I will if you will,"[9] but rather it is His covenant
people saying, "I will because You have." Are their consequences for
disobedience and blessings for obedience? Of course. Is this the heart
and motivation for the Law? No.

This formula of obedience as a relational response, as mentioned
earlier, is expressed in the prologue of the Decalogue. The opening
words can be summarised as follows: "Because I have rescued you…
because I am your God… this is how I want you to live." The Lord
would later reinforce this in Leviticus when He said, "I am the Lord
who brought you up out of the land of Egypt to be your God. You
shall *therefore* be holy, for I am holy" (Lev. 11:45). And again in Deuteronomy, through Moses, when He tells the people:

> You shall therefore love the Lord your God and keep his
> charge, his statutes, his rules, and his commandments
> always… And if you will indeed obey my commandments
> that I command you today, to love the Lord your God, and to

---

9   E.g. Andy Stanley, *Irresistible: Reclaiming the New that Jesus Unleashed for the World*
(Grand Rapids, MI: Zondervan, 2018), 33, 41, 135, 165, 181.

serve him with all your heart and with all your soul...
—Deuteronomy 11:1, 13

Obedience motivated by love is also why the Bible repeats the declaration that the Lord God "keeps covenant and steadfast love with those who *love him and keep his commandments*, to a thousand generations..." (Deut. 7:9; cf. Neh. 1:5; Dan. 9:7). Jesus reinforces this idea when He summarises the whole Law as loving God and loving neighbour (Matt. 22:37-40). And this was not some radical new combination either. In the Law are instructions on how to relate to God and how to relate to one's neighbour. Consider too the words of Micah: "He has told you, O man, what is good; and what does the LORD require of you but to do justice, and to love kindness, and to walk humbly with your God?" (Micah 6:8). Here, love for neighbour is expressed alongside love for God. In fact, much of this book of the Bible deals with this relationship in that God rejects their worship because of the way they treat the poor etc... Thus, even before Jesus, the connection between the vertical and horizontal was firmly in place. And although there are Laws that focus on one or the other, failure to love neighbour was a failure to love God, since He is the Lawgiver and creator of our neighbour. Thus, ultimately it is all about honouring and loving Him (Psalm 51:4). Therefore, when Jesus told His disciples "If you love me, you will keep my commandments" (John 14:15), it was ultimately a reference to His deity because His expectation is no different to what was expressed in the Tanakh, and the only foundation upon which He can give that instruction.

Again, a significant implication that we can take from this purpose of the Law is that it further reinforces the idea that God's purpose in giving the Law was that it was something to be obeyed, not merely some kind of diagnostic tool.

Social Order

The sixth key purpose of the Law, which was hinted at in the first purpose, is that the Law was given to bring the blessing of social order. It was not, as I have often heard, an unbearable yoke, nor is its purpose to curse. Yes, the consequence of disobedience involved and resulted in "curses," but that was a *consequence* for disobedience, not the intended *purpose*. Speed limits are set to keep drivers safe. If someone exceeds the posted speed and crashes their car, would we say it was the speed limit that did it? Should we say that we need to get rid of the speed limit to get rid of speeding? Of course not. Speed limits help protect other road uses and pedestrians as well as the individual driver. In the same way, the Law was given to protect the vulnerable and bring social blessing and flourishing. For example, as explained earlier, Moses says in Deuteronomy:

> I have set before you today life and good, death and evil. If
> you obey the commandments of the Lord your God that
> I command you today, by loving the Lord your God, by
> walking in his ways, and by keeping his commandments and
> his statutes and his rules, then you shall live and multiply,
> and the Lord your God will bless you in the land that you are
> entering to take possession of it.
> —Deuteronomy 30:15

God gave the Law so that His people would have wisdom and know how to live. And in keeping the Law, His people would bring life and flourishing to the covenant community. To see this in action, let's consider, for example, the judicial laws. The standards of evidence, namely two to three witnesses (or lines of evidence/testimony—Deut. 17:6), and the prospect of the punishment for the guilty being given to one who made a false accusation (Deut. 19:18-19), were there to protect the innocent from false punishment. Now, some might think, "What if they get away with it?" The Lord, the one who gave these divine Laws through Moses, as did His covenant people, had the worldview that if people got away with crimes in this life, they would definitely not get away with them in the next. The punishments themselves not only served as a deterrent to grossly sinning against one's neighbour, but also functioned to "make people whole." Lost property or loss of income due to injury was compensated by the guilty with interest, and if they were unable to pay, they were to be put to work until they could pay it off (Exodus 22:2-3). There was no jail or prison. If someone breaks into your home and steals your belongings, not only have you lost property that is of value, but repairs come with a cost too. Now imagine a situation where you are required to pay for the accommodation, meals, and supervision of a criminal as their penalty, and they give you nothing. That is the prison system. That doesn't make people whole. So, the Law's judicial provisions were a way to protect and bless the people materially.

The Law also blessed the people spiritually. Consider the prohibition against building idols and the instructions on building altars. Israel, like all people, had a problem with being enticed by idols. By prohibiting idolatry, others would be less likely to be tempted[10] and able to enjoy the blessings of true, devoted worship. In his article on the Sinai narrative, T.D. Alexander explains that these laws:

> focus on the important subject of how God's presence is to be
> experienced by the Israelites in the future. Yahweh's blessing
> will come to the people when they worship him through the

---

10   A principle Paul hints at in 1 Corinthians 8.

offering of sacrifices on altars, but not through the construction of golden or silver images.[11]

By keeping these Laws, it would ensure that the covenant people would experience the blessing of God's presence and commendation in their worship that would be lost had they bowed to the demons behind false deities.

The social benefits of obedience to the Law can also be seen in the way that social order and harmony was able to exist both as a blessing to the Israelites and as a witness to the nations. Therefore, considering these purposes, to go General Ackbar on the Law and call it "a trap"[12] is to ignore what Scripture says about it.

That the Law is a blessing on society is also seen in Paul's description of it as a guardian, or tutor, in Galatians 3. The tutor in the Greek and Roman world had little to do with teaching. Indeed, the idea of a tutor engaging in pedagogy and education is a later concept, originating around the 1300s. The tutor, or *paedagogus*, in Roman society, was a reliable slave who was involved in watching over children. They were charged with ethically training them through strict behaviour control and protecting them from the corrupt morals of society. As a guardian, the Law preserved God's people from a hostile world that would seek to corrupt them, and for three reasons:

One is to preserve the social and personal blessings that come through obedience to the commands to honour God and to love neighbour.

---

11 T.D. Alexander, "The Composition of the Sinai Narrative in Exodus XIX 1 – XXIV 11," *Vetus Testamentum*, 5-6.

12 Return of the Jedi. Lucasfilm. (1983).

Two is just as Noah was preserved through the flood to protect the line to the Messiah, Israel was likewise preserved in the world to bring forth the Messiah.

And three, as we saw earlier, was to preserve God's revelation of Himself and of the coming Messiah and His ministry.

Unfortunately, history shows that the Law's influence on the people in this role of keeping the nation from sin was not very successful. In Numbers 25, we read that many Israelites were led astray into Baal worship by the Moabites. Had they listened to their guardian, they would not have been corrupted. This is why Paul continues in Galatians 3 by saying that the Law as tutor leads us to our teacher, Christ.

As passages like Ezekiel 36:26-27 and Jeremiah 31:31-33 (which is cited in Hebrews 8:8-10) make clear, it takes more than an external force to keep people from sinning—it requires a heart change. This source of influence, and not content, is what Paul was referring to in Romans when he wrote: "having died to that which held us captive [sin], so that we serve in the new way of the Spirit and not in the old way of the [external *paedagogus*] written code" (Rom. 7:6). And according to Paul in Galatians 3, it is *this* specific, external influential *paedagogus* role of the Law that no longer applies to us as believers. In Galatians 3, when Paul said that "the law was our guardian until Christ came," he is not referring to the appearance of Christ in history in the incarnation. This is about the individual's encounter with Christ as seen in the remainder of the verse: "in order that we might be justified by faith. But now that faith has come, we are no longer under a guardian." When the individual encounters Christ and puts their faith in Him, they are justified, and the Law is written on their hearts in accordance with Jeremiah 31 and Ezekiel 36. If this passage was talking about Christ coming in history and thus ending the relevance of the Law with the inauguration of the New Covenant, then you must also say that justification by faith, and even faith in general, was non-existent before the First Century. But Genesis 15 and the accounting of righteousness for Abraham's faith clearly says otherwise. Thus, Galatians 3:23-25 is talking about the individual's experience of faith, not the moment of the incarnation.

Although God's Law becomes internalised by the Spirit, the external Word nonetheless still collaborates with the Holy Spirit to transform us. If all we need is the Spirit, and the external Word supposedly brings death, then perhaps we should throw out our Bibles. But we know that this is neither correct nor wise.

As we have seen, the purposes and goals of the Law are much more complex than simply to reveal sin, as is often argued. The Law has a multitude of roles and purposes, which means that even if one facet of the Law was superseded by something better, it does not render the entire Law irrelevant. Yet, that is how some approach it. Consider the iPhone, or perhaps the smartphone in general for those Android fans. This brilliant little invention is the Swiss-Army-Knife of entertainment, information, and communication technology. You can use it to make phone calls, write a book, read a book, find a recipe, listen to music, create a short film, watch a movie, send an email, play games, take photos, or even buy a car. Now, imagine that I believed that the only function my smartphone served was to watch YouTube. How do you believe that would affect the way I related to and thought about my phone, especially after realising that I can stream YouTube on my Smart TV, which has a screen that is far more superior? Of course, I would consider it irrelevant and redundant. I would tell people, "Why bother with your smart phone? There's something better! Throw it away!" All because I neglected its multiple purposes and uses. People do that with the Law. Now, of course, the analogy is not perfect, but to suggest that the whole Law has no relevance whatsoever is to ignore its multitude of purposes.

When we remember the eternal origins of the Law and the purposes of blessing that the Torah can bring, it should become evident that the Mosaic Covenant, therefore, was not a Covenant of Law with a new test of obedience, as Dispensationalism would claim. Grace was the foundation of God's relationship with His people from beginning to end. Moreover, the purpose of the Law was to paint a description of what it meant and looked like when the Lord called the people to be a Holy Nation and a Royal Priesthood, telling the people to be Holy as He is Holy.[13] This brings us to the conditional nature of the covenant.

---

13   F. Klooster, "The Biblical Method of Salvation: A Case for Continuity," *Continuity and Discontinuity* (Westchester: Crossway, 1988), np.

CHAPTER 3

A CONDITIONAL COVENANT

*"One of the marks of a good theologian is good thinking marked
by good distinctions based on the whole counsel of God."*[1]

When it comes to understanding Scripture, context is king. Both
the historical and textual settings help to shape the interpretation of
words, terms, and conditions. For example, some people cite Philippi-
ans 3:21 to demonstrate that all will be reconciled to Christ, without
exception. Yet, they ignore the words a couple of verses prior that say
that the ultimate destination of the enemies of the cross is destruction.
This also happens with some people's understanding of the nature of
the Law. Some may take a sample of verses, such as Paul's polemic
against justification by Works of the Law, and say that the New Covenant is incompatible in every way with the Old Covenant. I also
often hear people comparing and contrasting the "New Covenant"
with the "Mosaic Covenant" with phrases like: "The Old is about do
and the New is about done." And "Before Jesus, it was all about works,
but now it is all about grace," suggesting that the Mosaic Covenant
was about working for salvation and right standing with God. As an
example to show the irrelevance of the Old Testament to the Apostolic
Scriptures, Andy Stanley in his book Irresistible points the reader to
2 Chronicles 7:14. Here, Stanley explains that the promise in this
passage is God reiterating His conditional, reciprocal covenant that

---

1   Justin Taylor, "Are God's Covenants Conditional or Unconditional?" *The Gospel
     Coalition*, June 14, 2011, www.thegospelcoalition.org/blogs/justin-taylor/are-gods-
     covenants-conditional-or-unconditional/.

He made with Israel wherein which blessing required obedience.[2] And certainly, Exodus 19:5 does make the conditional statement, "if you will indeed obey my voice and keep my covenant, you shall be my treasured possession..." How, then are we to make sense of this? Was the Law given as a requirement of relationship and blessing, or was there something more?

Condition of Purpose

Answering these questions begins by recognising that the Mosaic Covenant is a vocational covenant. The whole covenantal declaration given by Moses in Exodus 19 says this:

> If you will indeed obey my voice and keep my covenant, you
> shall be my treasured possession among all peoples, for all the
> earth is mine; and you shall be to me a kingdom of priests
> and a holy nation.
> —Exodus 19:5-6

It is the final line that gives meaning to the conditional nature of the covenant.

Israel's function and purpose as a Kingdom of Priests and God's treasured people was to be a representative of the holiness, righteousness, and goodness of Yahweh to the nations. As was explained to Israel, they were to be a "light to the Gentiles" (Isaiah 42:6; 49:6; 60:3; cf. Deut. 4:6). This role was not new, rather, it was an articulation of the purpose for which people were created: to be reflections and representations of the image of God in the Earth. With

---

2   Andy Stanley, *Irresistible: Reclaiming the New that Jesus Unleashed for the World* (Grand Rapids, MI: Zondervan, 2018), 99-100.

this purpose in mind, the reader and hearer can make sense of the conditional language of Exodus 19. If they obey God's Law, then they will be functioning as God's covenant people. Thus, the details of the obligations to the Mosaic Covenant—the commandments, prohibitions and statutes expressed in the Torah—are descriptions of how Israel was to function in that vocation.

As a Holy Nation and kingdom of priests, it was Israel's role to distinguish between the holy and common (Ezekiel 44:23; Lev. 10:10-11). This meant living as those whose lives represent the one who not only separates order from chaos in creation, but also separates the holy from the common. This is seen in many of the commandments like the Sabbath and elements of what is referred to as the Holiness Code (Lev. 17-26), which dealt with matters such as sexuality, justice, standards of the priesthood, feast days, and redemption of property and people. Disobedience to God would consequently hinder that function as a witness of Yahweh to the nations. As Enns explains:

> Israel's obedience or disobedience to God's covenant stipulations has implications beyond simply that of Israel's relationship to God, that is blessing or curse. It has ramifications for the outworking of God's redemptive plan for the world.[3]

This is the essence of the conditional elements of the Mosaic Covenant. Namely, if the people do not obey His voice, then they are not functioning as a kingdom of priests.

Since the Mosaic Covenant is a vocational covenant, it is separate from the Covenant of Redemption, although there is some relationship. What this means is that the conditional statements are not about

---

3   Peter Enns, *Exodus* (Grand Rapids, MI: Zondervan 2000), 397.

entering that covenant, especially since the declaration of covenant obligations begins with the statement: "I *am* the Lord your God, who brought you out of the land of Egypt…" As descendants of Abraham, they were already His people. As God says in the beginning of Exodus, "I have surely seen the affliction of *my people* who are in Egypt" (Exod. 3:7), and "you shall say to Pharaoh, 'Thus says the Lord, *Israel is my firstborn son*, and I say to you, Let my son go that he may serve me'" (Exod. 4:22-23). This relationship as God's people is a fulfilment of the Lord's promise to Abraham in Genesis 17: "I will establish my covenant between me and you and your offspring after you throughout their generations for an everlasting covenant, to be God to you and to your offspring after you" (Gen. 17:7). Hence, obedience to the Law is not some condition for entrance into the covenant or for earning salvation; it is about living in that covenant. What this means is that obedience serves as a logical consequence of covenant membership: "If you are doing X Y Z, then you are functioning as a kingdom of priests, but more importantly, you are demonstrating that you are indeed my treasured possession." Thus, the fulfilment of covenant obligations is a by-product of being a genuine covenant member.

As Paul highlights in Romans 4, God elected, called, and promised descendants, land, and blessing to Abraham before He formally implemented any obligations. Just as the covenant of circumcision made with Abraham was a product of the relationship he had with the Lord, the Law was also to be a product of our relationship with God. This becomes evident when we consider the Hebrew grammar of the Ten Words. It was pointed out to me while listening to a podcast that the commandments do not use what is referred to as the imperative ("instructional") form. Instead, they use what is known as the "imperfect" form, which is used to describe an incomplete action or something that does happen in the present or will occur in the future.

For example, "students will be working now" or "we will be eating at 7." This is different to, "we must eat at 7." What this means is that the commands of the Ten Words are more like descriptions than they are instructions on how the people are to live. And this is true not only of the Ten Words but also of a significant portion of the commandments and statutes in the Law. However, it should be pointed out that the absence of the imperative form does not mean that the commandments are any less authoritative, nor does it detract from their instructional nature. It just helps us to highlight and reinforce the purpose of the Law as a description of how God's people are to live.

The implication of this understanding of the Law as a vocational description is that comparing the Mosaic Covenant with the New Covenant is kind of like comparing a mortgage contract with an insurance policy. Sure, there's a connection between the two in that you have insured items within the house you have mortgaged, but they deal with different matters for different purposes and outcomes.

Condition of Blessing

The other sense in which we find conditionality in the Mosaic covenant is with regards to blessings and curses. In Deuteronomy 28 we read:

> And if you faithfully obey the voice of the Lord your God,
> being careful to do all his commandments that I command
> you today, the Lord your God will set you high above all the
> nations of the earth. And all these blessings shall come upon
> you and overtake you, if you obey the voice of the Lord your
> God.
> —Deuteronomy 28:1-2

Following this passage is the explanation that the blessings for obedience are provision, protection, and possession of the land. Later in the same chapter, we read, "But if you will not obey the voice of the Lord your God or be careful to do all his commandments and his statutes that I command you today, then all these curses shall come upon you and overtake you" (Deut. 28:15). The curses, as explained in the following verses, were effectively the removal of those blessings for obedience.

The reason God blesses or curses Israel in response to their obedience or disobedience comes back to the vocational nature of the Mosaic Covenant. By conforming to their role as a Holy Nation that represents Yahweh's Holy Nature, God's blessing upon them glorifies Him. And should they fail to represent Him accurately, if God were to leave them unpunished after they persistently and unrepentantly continue sinning, His name would be shamed by the surrounding nations. As explained through the prophet Isaiah, Israel was refined by the exile for God's glory: "For my own sake, for my own sake, I do it, for how should my name be profaned?" (Isaiah 48:11). We also find the following words spoken through Malachi to the post-exilic priests: "If you will not listen, if you will not take it to heart to give honor to my name, says the Lord of hosts, then I will send the curse upon you and I will curse your blessings" (Malachi 2:2). Thus, discipline and curses are primarily about preserving the glory and honour of God's name. The same can be said of the blessings. As spoken through Isaiah to King Hezekiah: "I will defend this city to save it, for my own sake and for the sake of my servant David" (2 Kings 19:34). Here the Lord has vowed to protect Jerusalem, a promised blessing of the Mosaic Covenant, for the sake of His name and honour. In light of these examples, it should be clear that blessings and curses are ultimately about God honouring His name and His self-glorification. Why?

Because they are a witness to the surrounding nations, that they may know that Yahweh is God and come to experience the full blessings promised in the Abrahamic Covenant (Ezek. 29:21).

Condition of Promise

This language of blessings and curses in the Law is straight out of the Abrahamic Covenant. As the Lord told Abram in Genesis 12:3, "I will bless those who bless you, and curse those who curse you." What is interesting is that the promises given to Abram are reflected in the promises of blessing to Israel. And most of these promises were experienced in some degree by Abraham during his life. Thus, in order to experience the blessings of the Abrahamic Covenant—land, nationhood, and close relationship with the Lord—Abraham's descendants needed to walk blamelessly before their God and uphold their covenant obligations, just as their ancestor had to (Gen. 17). At a glance, this appears to be a case of having to obey to be blessed, making it a covenant based on works, but it is actually no different than how one understands obedience as an obligation in the New Covenant (John 14:15; cf. Deut. 5:10). While I deal with this issue more deeply in *Forgotten Covenant*,[4] the essence of this condition is similar to that mentioned above in the section "Condition of Purpose." Namely, that "it is those who have genuine faith that brings one into true relationship with God and [therefore] diligent to demonstrate that faith that will experience the fullness of those blessings."[5] Therefore, obedience as an obligation does not affect the unconditionally of God's promises to Abraham. Disobedience only annulled the blessings for individuals and generations because their *continuous* rebellion is a demonstration

---

4   See R.L. Watson, *Forgotten Covenant* (Port Orchard, WA: Ark House Press, 2021), 76-82.
5   Ibid., 81.

of the lack of faith that would have prevented a genuine relationship with the Lord. Therefore, the conditionality of the Mosaic Covenant as a fulfilment of the Abrahamic Covenant was about "the quality of life lived in the promise and the joy of participating in all the benefits of that promise."[6] To go back to the swimming analogy: if you don't get in the pool, you won't get wet.

It is also important to note that the conditionality of blessing upon obedience was only about the greater material blessings of the covenant. As Jesus said, God "makes his sun rise on the evil and on the good, and sends rain on the just and on the unjust" (Matt. 5:45).

When reading about the blessings and curses in the Law, some Christians correspond these with salvation and damnation, concluding that the Mosaic Covenant was about justification by obedience. The blessings, as we have seen, were about the experience of the *material* promises made with Abraham, not salvation. Genuine obedience was a sign they are already enjoying the promised *spiritual* blessings. As Old Testament Professor William Barrick explains, God had

> redeemed [Israel] before He entered the covenant with them at Sinai. Any claim that the covenant needed to be kept in order for someone to be saved from sin denies the theological and redemptive contexts of the Mosaic Covenant historically.[7]

So, was the "Old Covenant" a conditional covenant that required obedience for blessings? Well, kind of. But this needs to be understood in light of the covenant's context. Moreover, we cannot say that it is

---

6   Walter Kaiser, "God's Promise Plan and His Gracious Law," *JETS*, 294.

7   William Barrick, "The Mosaic Covenant," *The Masters Seminary Journal*, 10/2 (1999), 220.

the sole formula for the totality of all aspects of Israel's relationship with Yahweh.

As we have seen, obedience to the Law under the Mosaic Covenant was a requirement to function as God's Holy Nation, much in the same way that eating meat is a requirement to be a carnivore. It was also a requirement to experience the material blessings of the Abrahamic Covenant as a proclamation of God's glory to the nations that they may know Him. Moreover, true obedience is a demonstration of the genuine relationship that comes by grace through faith. And those who are in that relationship will experience these gracious blessings anyway. This is no different from James saying that "faith without works is dead," and that Abraham's faith was "vindicated"[8] by his works. Therefore, to try to draw a contrast between the New Covenant and the Mosaic Covenant is both unreasonable since they served different purposes. But it is also inaccurate because grace is the foundation of both.

---

8   From the Gk *edikaiothe* in James 2:21. Although often translated as justified, within this textual context the word vindicate is a valid and theologically consistent translation.

CONCLUSION

WHY THEN THE LAW?

In light of what the Bible says about the Law, how do we answer the question, *Why then the Law?* Quite simply, since the Law's origins are found in the eternal nature of God, we can begin to recognise that it is more than "a temporal, Jewish thing." Since God is the creator of the Jew and the Gentile, the Law of God is universal and will be applied universally. It will silence people of all nations who on the Day of Judgement (Rom. 3:19) would try to say "But God…"

We can also see that the purposes of the Law are much more complex and dynamic than merely showing peoples' unrighteousness and guilt. Although that is still a significant and relevant purpose with regards to the Gospel, it should also become apparent that it is God's intention that His creatures and image-bearers keep His Law. Not in order to merit favour or salvation, but rather:

- to glorify the Lord by revealing God's righteous and holy character to the nations,
- to demonstrate love and gratitude to the Lord, and
- to bring blessing and flourishing to society.

Hopefully now, having considered the nature and purpose of the Law according to scripture, when we read about God's Law we can move beyond overly simplistic caricatures and descriptions of the Law as bondage, burden, curse, and slavery. We can recognise that the Law is contrary to the Gospel only if one were trying to be justified by it.

Nonetheless, there is actually a stronger relationship between the Law and the Gospel than one may think. Jeremiah 31 provides a description that shows this close relationship:

Behold, the days are coming, declares the Lord, when I will make a new covenant with the house of Israel and the house of Judah, not like the covenant that I made with their fathers on the day when I took them by the hand to bring them out of the land of Egypt, my covenant that they broke, though I was their husband, declares the Lord. *For this is the covenant that I will make with the house of Israel after those days, declares the Lord: I will put my law within them, and I will write it on their hearts.* And I will be their God, and they shall be my people.
—Jeremiah 31:31-33

Ezekiel 36 paints a similar picture too:

I will vindicate the holiness of my great name, which has been profaned among the nations, and which you have profaned among them. And the nations will know that I am the Lord, declares the Lord God, when through you I vindicate my holiness before their eyes. I will take you from the nations and gather you from all the countries and bring you into your own land. I will sprinkle clean water on you, and you shall be clean from all your uncleannesses, and from all your idols I will cleanse you. And I will give you a new heart, and a new spirit I will put within you. And I will remove the heart of stone from your flesh and give you a heart of flesh. *And I will put my Spirit within you, and cause you to walk in my statutes and be careful to obey my rules.*
—Ezekiel 36:23-27

In both these passages, as a fulfilment of the Lord's plan of redemption through the New Covenant, we are told that God's Law, with its statutes and rules, becomes written on our hearts so that we can do them. We are guilty of sin, and we fail to obey God because our fallen nature causes us to rebel and break His eternal Law. This is lawlessness, and the definition of sin mentioned earlier which in Greek is written as *anomia*.[1] To live *anomia* means to live as though God's Law does not exist or has no authority over us. Thus, to redeem His people from the consequences of the fall, He doesn't merely forgive, but He transforms us and sanctifies us by the Holy Spirit, changing us from the inside out. Paul expressed this in Romans 8 when he wrote,

> ...those who live according to the flesh set their minds on the things of the flesh, but those who live according to the Spirit set their minds on the things of the Spirit. For to set the mind on the flesh is death, but to set the mind on the Spirit is life and peace. For the *mind that is set on the flesh is hostile to God, for it does not submit to God's law; indeed, it cannot.* Those who are in the flesh cannot please God.
> —Romans 8:5-8

Therefore, rather than being opposed to the Gospel, genuine, Spirit-empowered obedience to God's Law is a fulfilment of the Gospel. What extent of the Law applies to Christians today is a topic bigger than the purposes of this small book, but it should be sufficient to say that it has more significance and relevance for followers of Christ today than some may believe.

---

1   Found in passages such as Matt 7:23¬¬¬, 13:41, 2Cor 6:14, 1Jn 3:4.

And in light of this relevance between the Law and the Gospel, it should become apparent that the giving of the Law at Sinai was not an isolated part of salvation history that needs to be contained within the Tanakh at all cost. Rather, the revelation of the Law in the Mosaic Covenant demonstrates that it is a significant expression and component of God's restoration of humanity's vocation in creation, which He began through Abraham. And as with Abraham, the covenant obligations of the Law are a product of and not a foundation for one's relationship with God.

BIBLIOGRAPHY

Alexander, T. "The Composition of the Sinai Narrative in Exodus XIX 1-XXIV 11." *Vetus Testamentum*. XLIX. (1999): 5-6.

Barrick, William. "The Mosaic Covenant." *The Masters Seminary Journal*. 10/2 (1999). p213-232.

Childs, Brevard. 2004. *The Book of Exodus*. Louisville: Westminster John Knox Press.

Craigie, Peter. 1976. *The Book of Deuteronomy*, NICOT. Grand Rapids: Eerdmans.

Enns, Paul. 2000. *Exodus: The NIV Application Commentary*. Grand Rapids: Zondervan.

Griffiths, Phillip. 2016. *Covenant Theology: A Reformed Baptist Perspective*. Eugene: WIPF.

Hegg, Timothy. 2013. *Paul's Epistle to the Galatians*. Tacoma: Torah Resource.

Jeffrey, Steve, Ovey, Mike, Sach, Andrew. 2007. *Pierced for our Transgressions*. Nottingham: IVP.

Kaiser, Walter. "God's Promise Plan and his Gracious Law." *Journal of the Evangelical Theological Society* 33 (Sept 1990): 294.

Klooster, F. 1988. "The Biblical Method of Salvation: A Case for Continuity," *Continuity and Discontinuity*. Edited by John Feinberg, np. Westchester: Crossway. Accessed on books.google.com.

Krebs, Albin. "Gene Kelly, Dancer of Vigor and Grace, Dies." New York Times, February 3, 1996.

Luther, Martin. 1998. *Commentary on the Epistle to the Galatians*. *Trans*. Theodore Graebner. Kindle.

Ryrie, Charles. 2007. *Dispensationalism*. Chicago: Moody Press.

Sproul, R.C. "The Covenant." *Ligonier Ministries*. Feb, 2017. www.ligonier.org/learn/sermons/covenant

Stanley, Andy. 2018. *Irresistible: Reclaiming the New that Jesus Unleashed for the World*. Grand Rapids: Zondervan.

Stephens, Wallace. Sourced from:quoterati.com/authors/ wallace-stevens.

Taylor, Justin. "Are God's Covenants Conditional or Unconditional?" *The Gospel Coalition* (US). June 14, 2011. Sourced: www.thegospelcoalition.org/blogs/justin-taylor/are-gods-covenants-conditional-or-unconditional/

Watson, R.L. 2021. *Forgotten Covenant*. Mona Vale: Arkhouse Press.

ABOUT THE AUTHOR
R. L. WATSON

Theology matters because a good, strong, biblical theology is what empowers believers to worship God in spirit and in truth with all our being, and allows us to endure the material, emotional and spiritual trials of life. Motivated by this reality, Ryan Watson is an author and Bible teacher committed to equipping Christians to build a theology with an all-of-scripture (Tota Scriptua) way of interpreting the Bible, and helping followers of Christ to understand the historical and linguistic context of the Word. He is also passionate about helping readers of Scripture recognise the goodness, sovereignty, and glory of God and the beauty of His Gospel.

Ryan has both undergraduate and post-graduate qualifications in Theology after studying under the Australian College of Theology at Malyon College in Brisbane, Australia. He has experience in preaching, teaching, and has served as a Youth Pastor. At the University of Queensland, he studied a BA with majors in Ancient and Modern History and English, and has completed a Graduate Diploma of Education.

As well as completing this, his first book, Ryan has written *Forgotten Covenant* (2021), which explores the Abrahamic Covenant and the biblical narrative, and *Let no one Judge You* (2022), which is a part of the Pronomian Pocketbook Series that looks at the heresy described in Colossians 2. Ryan has published essays on academia.edu, including one about the typology of Melchizadek in Hebrews. He has also written a number of blog articles, which are available on his website.

Ryan lives in Brisbane, Australia with his wife and four boys, and works as a High-School English teacher.

www.ingramcontent.com/pod-product-compliance
Lightning Source LLC
Chambersburg PA
CBHW060041050426
42448CB00012B/3101